This book belongs to a poet called:

For all the young writers who've tried their hand at poetry in my creative writing workshops. Here's some of what you've taught me! – S.T.

*First published 2024 by Walker Books Ltd
87 Vauxhall Walk, London SE11 5HJ*

*2 4 6 8 10 9 7 5 3 1
Text © 2024 Sean Taylor
Illustrations © 2024 Sam Usher*

The right of Sean Taylor and Sam Usher to be identified as the author and illustrator respectively of this work has been asserted in accordance with the Copyright, Designs and Patents Act 1988

This book has been typeset in Stempel Schneidler

Printed in China

All rights reserved. No part of this book may be reproduced, transmitted or stored in an information retrieval system in any form or by any means, graphic, electronic or mechanical, including photocopying, taping and recording, without prior written permission from the publisher.

*British Library Cataloguing in Publication Data:
a catalogue record for this book is available from the British Library*

ISBN 978-1-5295-1406-3

www.walker.co.uk

You're a POET
Ways to Start Writing Poems

Sean Taylor   illustrated by Sam Usher

"Poetry is a bucket for holding truth"
Adrian Mitchell

In poems there is freshness.

In poems there is song.

In poems there's no right.

In poems there's no wrong.

CONTENTS

Piglet ... You're a Poet .... Page 6

As Loud As Thunder Booming! .... Page 18

The Breeze Is My Friend .... Page 32

If I Was a Tree .... Page 46

I Would Give You .... Page 58

Piglet ... You're a Poet

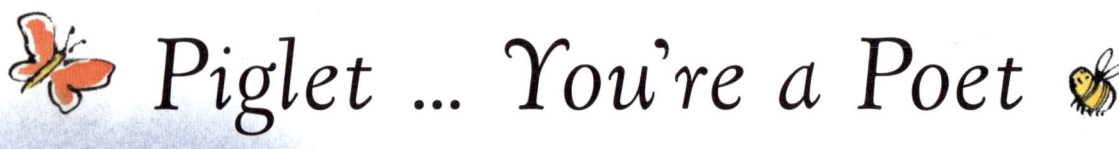

It was bright. It was warm.

And Piglet's mum said it would be
a good day to go for a walk up the hill.

As they set off along the puddly track,
the two of them seemed happy
for no particular reason at all.

And when Piglet picked up a stone
and dropped it in a puddle,
something special happened.

Words splashed out of the water.

Piglet said them:

SUNSHINY EARTHY WET PUDDLE
FRESH SPLOSHING

Mum told him, "Piglet … that's a poem!"

That put a pleased look on Piglet's face.
But it was also a bit of a *wondering-what* look.
And he asked his mum, "*Why* is it a poem?"
Mum laughed and told him, "I don't know
if I can say. I just know what a poem is
when I hear one!"

The track went winding through the woods
and on to the meadow with the sandpit.

Sometimes when they went there
the sandpit looked damp and grey.
But today it was dry and it was golden.

So Piglet jumped in.
And something special happened.

Words splashed out of the sand.

Piglet said them:

WARM
SWISHING
LOOSE
SOFT
DEEP
SAND

He looked up at his mum and he asked,
"Is that a poem too?"
"That's a poem!" said Mum. "It's just a few words, but they're *true* words."

On up the hill they walked.

Up.

On.

Up.

Then, at the top, they stood next to each other and caught their breath. There was the meadow below. There was the sandpit, the woods and the puddly track leading home.

And Piglet suddenly said, "Let's ROLY-POLY down…"

Off he went. And Mum went with him!
They roly-polyed round and round and round
and down. And something special happened.
Words splashed out of Mum.

Piglet called them out:

BIG
BRAVE
ROUND AND ROUND
LAUGHING
LOVING
MUM!

They were zig-zaggy with how dizzy they'd got.

"Those words were true words!" said Piglet.
Mum nodded. "They were true words for you.
And they made me feel something true too!"

Piglet was still spin, spin, spinning
from the rolling round. Even his feet
were dizzy! But that was all right.
It was an exciting kind of being dizzy.

His mum looked as if she had a smile in her heart, not just on her face. And she said,

"Piglet ... you're a poet!"

A PUDDLE POEM

When he went for the walk with his mum, Piglet made up three short poems. They are what you could call 'puddle poems'.

Would you like to try writing one?

If so,
first draw a circle.
That's your puddle.

Then decide what your poem is going to be about, and write it in the middle of the puddle.

You could write CITY or FOREST or THE SEA or SUMMER or THE MOON or anything else you like.

How about a puddle poem about FIRE?

Next, imagine dropping
a stone into your puddle, and draw
some splashes. Five splashes might be
a good number to start with.
But it could be more or less:

Now, what describing
words splash out from your puddle?
Here are some which could splash out
to describe FIRE:

To read your puddle poem,
start with the words round the outside,
then finish with what's written in the middle.

So the FIRE puddle poem goes:

HOT

SMOKY

RED, ORANGE, YELLOW

CRACKLING

DANCING

FIRE

WRITING SECRETS

If you want, you can write more than one word for each splash. Fire isn't just red. It's several colours. So in the fire puddle poem there are several words for that splash –
RED, ORANGE, YELLOW.

Remember all of your senses when picking words to splash out. If the FIRE poem only described what fire *feels* like, it wouldn't be very interesting. Instead, there's a word for what fire smells like (SMOKY), there's a word for what fire sounds like (CRACKLING) and there's a word for how fire moves (DANCING). A mix of many kinds of describing words will help your poem come to life!

 As Loud As Thunder Booming!

Piglet and Squirrel were best friends. So when Piglet's family went on holiday, they took Squirrel too.

Squirrel does everything quickly.
She eats quickly.

She runs quickly.
She speaks quickly.

"Are we … are we … are we going to sleep in a tent?" she asked.
Piglet gave a happy nod.

"Will we ... will we be by the sea?"
"Right by the sea," Piglet told her.

"And can we jump in and splash, splash, splash, splash, splash, splash, SPLASH?"
"Yes, yes, yes, yes, yes, yes, YES!" said Piglet.

He jumped up and down as he said it. Both of them jumped up and down – as if they were already there.

But then they arrived, and the wind seemed to be blowing from all directions at once.

They went to the beach, and the sea was wild. Great green and white waves were rumbling and crashing.

"It's so LOUD!" shouted Piglet.

"AS LOUD AS THUNDER BOOMING!"

called out Dad.

So it was all right to race around, dig in the sand and eat ice cream while watching the waves. But nobody could go in the water.

The wind blew until evening. It blew so much, in the end it blew itself away. And the sky cleared.

So when they got to the beach the next morning, everything was still. And Piglet and Squirrel *could* jump in the sea.

They ran. They dived. They splash, splash, splash, splash, SPLASHED!

When they'd had enough,
they lay down, feeling tired.

Squirrel said,
"It was so loud yesterday."
"It was as loud as a stomping monster!" said Piglet.
"Or as loud as a truck in a tunnel!" smiled Squirrel.
"As loud as a tiger roaring!" said Piglet.
"As loud as a wild wind whirling!" called out Squirrel.

"But it's all quiet now," went on Piglet.

"As quiet as a baby breathing," said Squirrel.

"As quiet as an apple on a branch," said Piglet, softly.

"As quiet as a feather falling onto sand," said Squirrel, more softly still.

"As quiet as the moon rising in the night," whispered Piglet.

Then Piglet said, "That might probably be a *poem* we've invented."

"I know, I know," nodded Squirrel. "Because they're wondering, wandering words we've thought up."

And she remembered all the words:

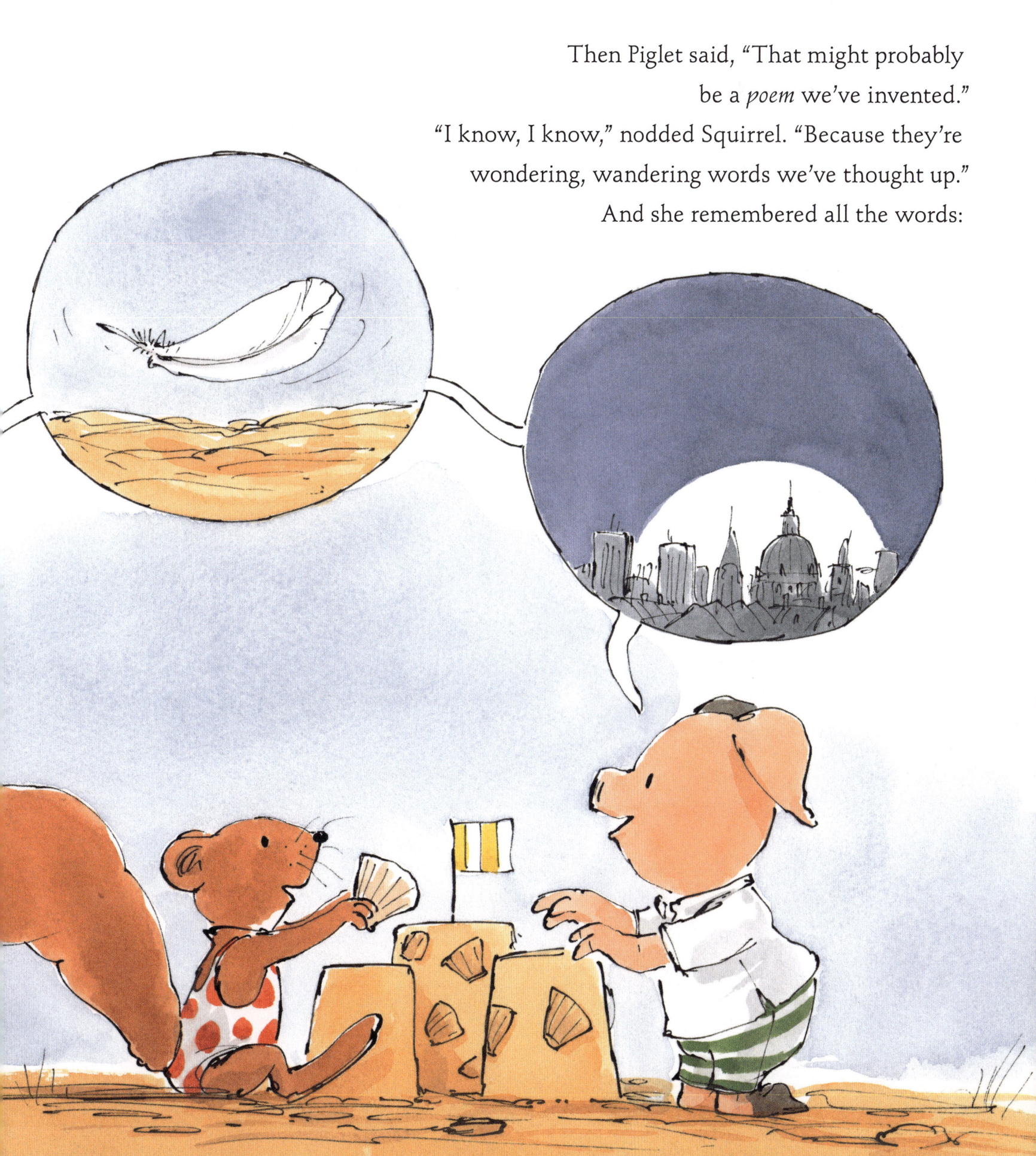

"As loud as a stomping monster!
As loud as a truck in a tunnel!
As loud as a tiger roaring!
As loud as a wild wind whirling!

As quiet as a baby breathing.
As quiet as an apple on a branch.
As quiet as a feather falling onto sand.
As quiet as the moon rising in the night."

"It *definitely* might probably be a poem," said Piglet.

Squirrel got up, because she didn't like lying down feeling tired for too long. Then she said, "And I think it definitely might probably be the best poem ever written by a piglet and a squirrel, on holiday by the sea!"

A COMPARING POEM

Here's another poetry adventure you can go on. How about inventing a COMPARING poem, like Piglet and Squirrel?

In their poem, they described a stormy sea by comparing it to things that are loud. Squirrel, for example, thought it was:
As loud as a wild wind whirling!

Then they described a calm sea by comparing it to things that are quiet. Piglet, for example, said it was:
As quiet as an apple on a branch.

Comparing things like this is fun. And it makes writing exciting, because the words create pictures in your mind!

Here are some other 'word pictures' made by comparing:

As tall as a tower

As hard as a bone

As green as a frog

You can have some fun by writing a comparing poem like Piglet and Squirrel. Choose a pair of opposites. They don't have to be LOUD and QUIET. Other opposites could be just as good for making a poem.

You might like one of these:

AS BRIGHT AS... /
AS DARK AS...

AS LIGHT AS... /
AS HEAVY AS...

AS QUICK AS... /
AS SLOW AS...

Or you might come up with a completely different pair of opposites.

Whatever opposites you choose, think up four ways of comparing one of them, then four ways of comparing the other.

If you choose AS QUICK AS and AS SLOW AS, the lines of the first verse can start like this:

As quick as...

As quick as...

As quick as...

As quick as...

Finish those lines by thinking up four interesting things that are quick.

The lines of the second verse can start like this:

As slow as...

As slow as...

As slow as...

As slow as...

Finish those lines by thinking up four interesting things that are slow.

Then you've got a poem.

WRITING SECRETS

Try to vary the things you compare with. Piglet and Squirrel's poem wouldn't be so interesting if they just compared the sea with a noisy tiger, a noisy rhinoceros and nothing except noisy animals!

Don't choose the most obvious things to compare with. Try to think up things that will take us by surprise. Instead of, As cold as ice, how about, As cold as a greyhound's nose?!

Comparing creates a picture in your mind. So make the picture as clear as possible. If Piglet had said: As loud as a monster! we wouldn't know *how* the monster was loud. Was it singing? Was it banging on a wall? Piglet actually says: As loud as a stomping monster! That gives us a clear picture.

Piglet and Squirrel wrote their poem together. Would you like to try writing a poem together with someone else? Perhaps that will add to the fun.

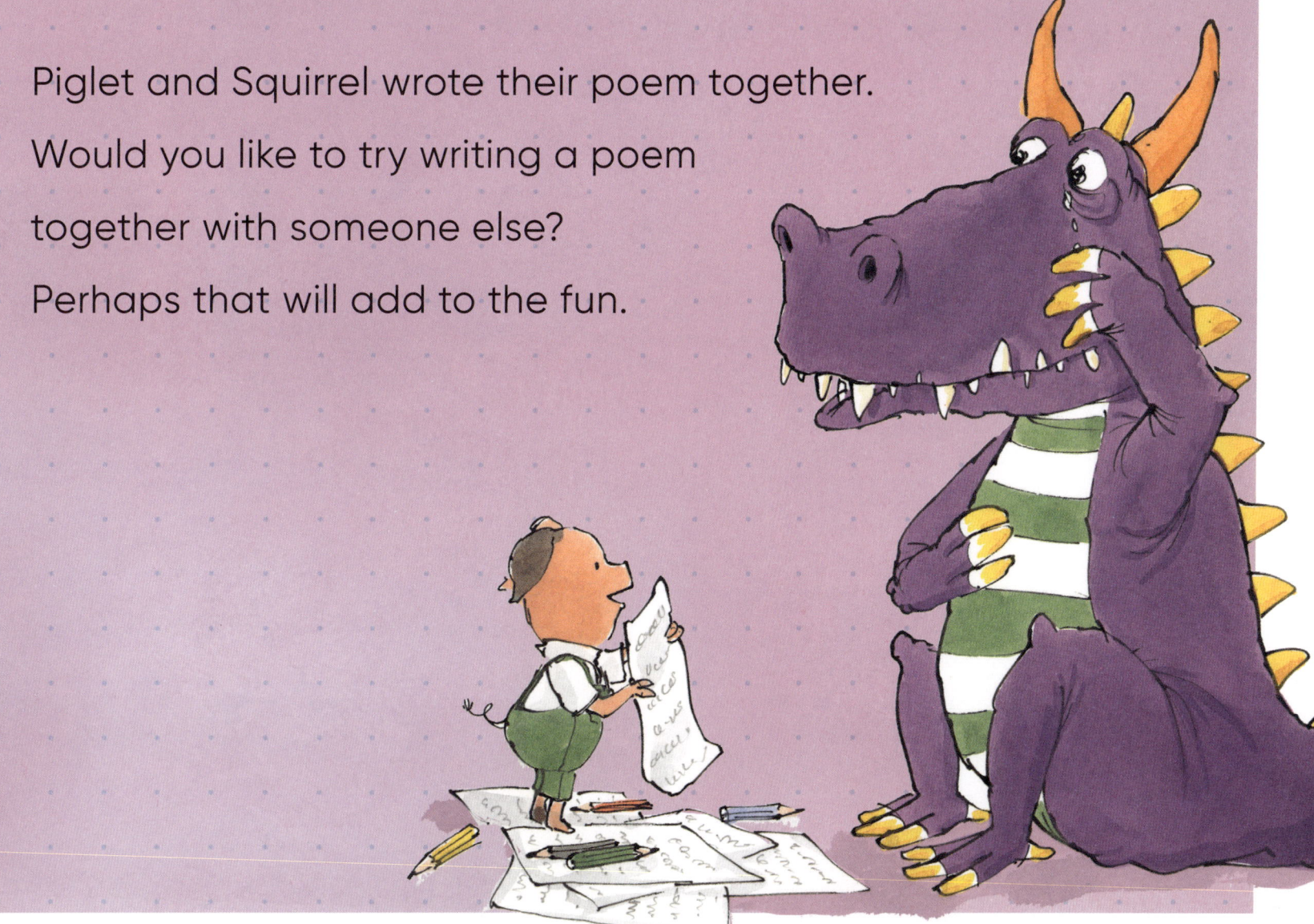

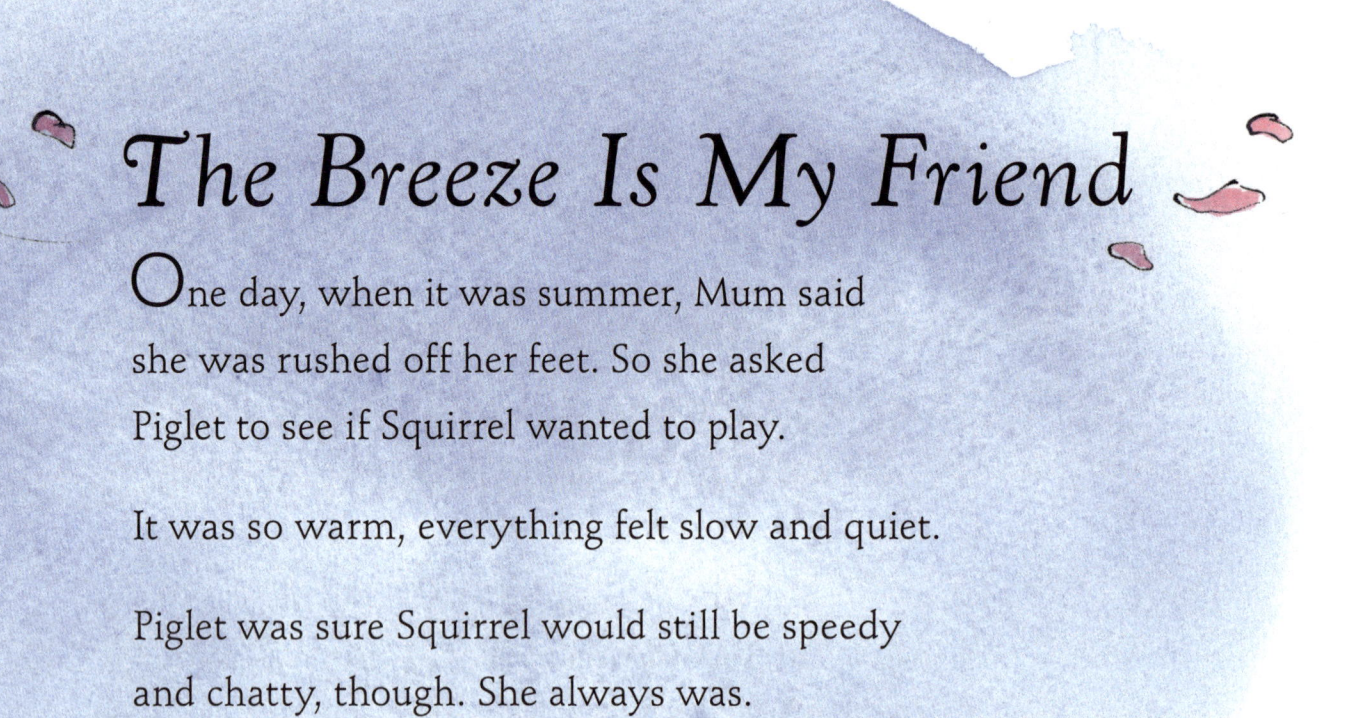

The Breeze Is My Friend

One day, when it was summer, Mum said she was rushed off her feet. So she asked Piglet to see if Squirrel wanted to play.

It was so warm, everything felt slow and quiet.

Piglet was sure Squirrel would still be speedy and chatty, though. She always was.

But it turned out Squirrel was asleep!
Her dad said she'd been awake
in the night because it was so hot.
And now she was having a nap.

Piglet wasn't in the mood to wait until Squirrel
woke up. But he wasn't in the mood to go home either.
So he walked halfway. Then he stopped by a tree.

There was a small and sad question in his head.
He asked it out loud.
"What am I going to do, when there's nothing to do?"

And, straight away, he heard a whispering kind of answer.

It was the breeze, in the leaves and the trees.
It blew blossom in the air. And Piglet reached out.
He tried to catch some petals.

The blossom danced around too fast.
So Piglet couldn't catch it.

But the breeze came again, as if it thought the game was good.

More petals flew.
Piglet jumped.

He caught one!
He caught two!
He caught three!

He played until
he was hot and thirsty.

Then Piglet sat down. The breeze was cool on his face. And he said to himself, "The breeze is my friend."

That seemed like maybe it was the start of a poem. So he closed his eyes, in a looking-for-words sort of way.

And he kept on,

The breeze is my friend.
He skips around
without any shoes.

The breeze is my friend.
He plays and plays and
plays and plays.

The breeze is my friend.
He whispers,
"Catch me if you can!"

The breeze is my friend.
I can't see him smiling
but I know that he is!

Piglet looked around and blinked,
almost as if he was waking up,
but his dream was a poem.

And he could hear a sound he recognized.
It was Squirrel laughing. So he headed back
the way he'd come.

At Squirrel's house, Piglet said, "That's good. You're *here* now."

"I must be, if we're looking at each other." Squirrel smiled. "And it's good you're here, because you can get wet in the sprinkler and have lemonade with me!"

The sprinkler squirted water this way and that.
The two friends ran through it about 116 times.

Then Squirrel's dad gave them lemonade. And Piglet's mum came along. So she had lemonade too.

Squirrel was hopping with happiness.
"I love being us!" she said.

Piglet loved being them too.

He loved playing with his happy friend.

But he also remembered playing with the breeze, and making up a poem about it.

MAKING-A-PERSON-OUT-OF-SOMETHING POEM

When Piglet went to Squirrel's house, she was having a nap. So he ended up playing with the breeze. And he made up a poem about it.

The breeze isn't alive. But in the poem, Piglet imagines that it is. He describes the breeze as a friend doing things and feeling things.

This is a good way to make a poem full of life and description. And if you want, you can write a poem like Piglet's.

First think up a subject for your poem. It needs to be something that isn't a person. But it needs to be something that you could describe as if it were a person.

Here are some ideas:

Could you describe a SEESAW as a person?

How about SUNSHINE?
What kind of human being would sunshine be?

What if your BED was a person?
What would they be like?

Those are some suggestions. You may have other ideas.
Just think and look around. Then, when you've chosen a subject,
describe what kind of person your subject is.

What MOOD are they in?

What are they DOING?

What are they WEARING?

What do they SAY?

What makes them DIFFERENT to other people?

Piglet starts each verse of his poem with the same words:

The breeze is my friend...

You can do that if you want.
Or you can start each verse in a new way.
It doesn't matter.

You just need to write down things that you imagine, and it will be a poem!

WRITING SECRETS

If you want, you can try making a person out of something that you can't see or touch. For example, what kind of person would *Sunday* be? What kind of person would *Monday* be? Or how about writing about a feeling? What kind of person would *worry* be? What kind of person would *calmness* be?

Have a bit of a think before you start. Try daydreaming a bit about the poem you want to write. It may come out quite differently to the way you expect. That's normal with poems. But a bit of thinking will help you get started.

If I Was a Tree

When it was a Saturday, Piglet and his dad found a rope. Dad said, "That would be just right for a swing."

So they went into the wood.

"Where's a swing going to go?" asked Piglet. "We want a branch that's strong, high and straight," Dad told him. And the two of them wandered away, not very fast and not very straight.

Piglet spotted a branch that was strong and high. But it wasn't straight. Dad spotted a branch that was high and straight. But it wasn't strong.

Then Piglet said, "That's what we want!" Dad agreed.

It was straight. It was strong. And it was high. He showed Piglet how to tie a loop. Then it took three tries, but Piglet threw the loop over the branch.

The rest was easy.

And Squirrel came along.

Her bright eyes blinked up. "Why … why … why … are you tying a rope to a tree?" she asked. "A tree can't run away!"

Piglet chuckled. "It's a swing."

"We just need a piece of wood for the seat," added Dad.

So they looked.

And they decided on a strong, little plank.

"I'M GOING FIRST!" Piglet and Squirrel said, both at the same time. "Well," Dad told them, "if you sit one on each side, I think you can *both* go first!"

They could! Off, up and away they went,
leaving a trail of laughter in the air.

They swung and swung. Everyone had a turn.
Even Dad!

Piglet was good at running and jumping on.
It made him go so high that
Squirrel jiggled with excitement.

And, as Piglet glided that way and this,
he looked up. And he had a poem idea.

It started:

"If I was a tree..."
Every time he swung back, he thought up
a line. And every time he swung forwards,
he called it out:

"If I was a tree, I'd be a small one in a big wood.
I'd be outside, even when there was a storm.
All kinds of birds would come and sing in me!
If I was a tree, I'd be the greenest green you've seen.
I'd have a branch that's strong and high and straight.
And friends would always come and swing from me!"

Dad gave a laugh.

"How did you make that up?" he asked.

"I don't know," said Piglet.

"I just thought of the best words to say what I was feeling."

Squirrel nodded and said,

"That is a true fact about how to write a poem."

"Well, I've got to say, I'm glad
you made it up, Piglet," Dad told him.
"That was like some music made of words."
Squirrel added, "And I've got to say, if you
were a tree, Piglet, and *I wasn't a tree*,
I would always come and swing from you!"

Piglet jumped down. And a while later
the three of them wandered back,
not very fast and not very straight.

AN IF-I-WAS POEM

How about writing a poem about yourself this time?

Piglet imagines himself as a tree. You could do that.
If you were a tree, what kind of tree would you be?

You could start your poem, like he does, with the words:
If I was a tree...
Then maybe you could think of four, five or six things about the tree that you would be.

Or you might imagine yourself as something else.

Here are some other suggestions for first lines:

If I was a boat...

If I was a colour...

If I was a musical instrument...

When you've chosen your first line, see what happens! That's what Piglet does. He calls out six different things about the tree that he would be.

He describes what size he would be:

He thinks up things that would happen to him:

And he describes what he would look like:

> If I was a tree, I'd be a small one in a big wood.

> I'd be outside, even when there was a storm.

> If I was a tree, I'd be the greenest green you've seen.

Every line says something about what the tree is like.
And it says something about what Piglet is like.

You could do the same. Imagine yourself as a tree, or something else — and make it a poem that tells us something about who you are.

How many lines should the poem have? It's up to you.
Maybe four or five lines. Maybe six lines, like Piglet's poem.
And you never know, you might find you write
ten lines ... or more!

WRITING SECRETS

Whatever you're describing, put in some detail.
If you're imagining yourself as a tree, like Piglet does,
tell us what makes it different to any other tree in the world.

The lines of Piglet's poem are all about the same length.
This gives the poem a nice flowing rhythm. Maybe you
can write words with some kind of rhythm too.

Have another think about your poem, after it is finished. Are there any words that could be better? If there are, you can change them. Making changes to a poem often improves it. Try out new words. And if the new words could *still* be better, then change them too!

I Would Give You

It was a damp sort of morning. Rain kept starting, then stopping, then starting again.

Piglet said, "Mum, I want to wear my *favourite* T-shirt."

"That needs washing," Mum told him.

Piglet gave her a grumpy look.
And he shouted, **"I'VE ALWAYS *NOT GOT IT* BECAUSE YOU *ALWAYS NEVER WASH IT!*"**

Mum said, "Well, I wasn't thinking about washing clothes. I was thinking a rainy day is what we need to paint your bedroom. We've been wanting to do that for a long time."

It was true. They had.

So, when he was dressed,
Piglet looked at different colours.

And he didn't want green.
He didn't want yellow.
But he *did* want blue.
And Mum said, "That'll look just right."

Then they started work.
And one wall began to be blue.

It was slow. But Mum kept painting and painting.
Piglet helped. It didn't matter if he painted
a blue boat, a blue sea and even a blue sun.
Because each wall went all blue, in the end.

And when they finished, it didn't look just right.

It looked *better* than just right!

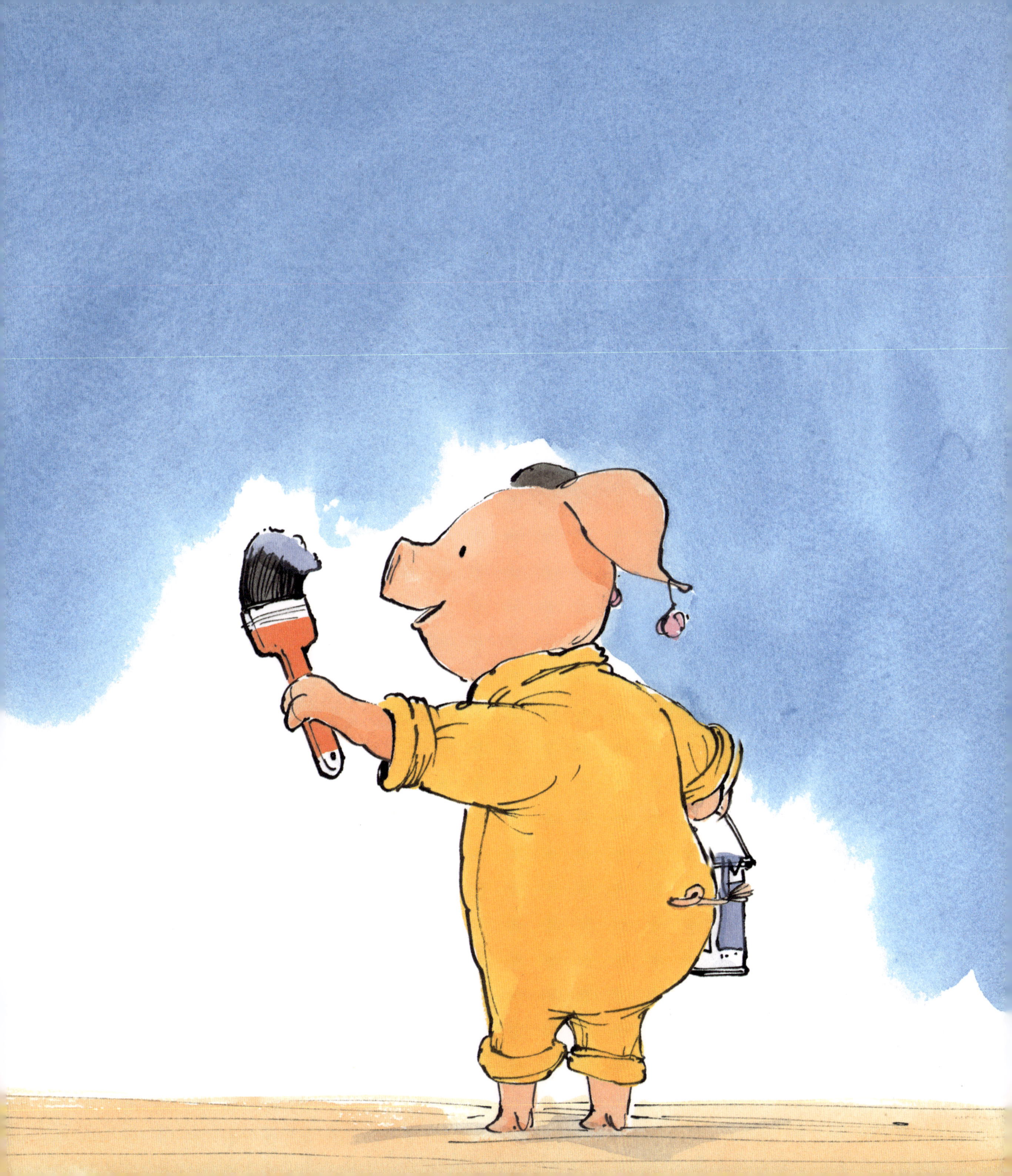

Mum said, "You've got paint all over you, Piglet.
It's lucky you weren't wearing your favourite T-shirt!"

That made Piglet give her a hug.
He was sorry about being grumpy in the morning.

The hug was as warm as a glove.
But he wanted to give her some kind of
thank you surprise, too.

He thought of making her tea with ginger biscuits.
But he couldn't reach up.

He thought of giving her a flower.
But he went out and there weren't any flowers.

So he decided he didn't have anything to give.

But as he was thinking that thought,
there were words in his head.

I would give you.

The words started an idea. A poem could
be a thank you. And it could be a surprise.
It could be *lots of surprises*!

So, word by word, Piglet made a poem.

Then he found Mum and read it to her,

"I would give you a cup of tea
with ginger biscuits.

I would give you funny jokes
to make you smile.

I would give you a day with
nothing to do.

I would give you the smell in the woods
when it's summer.

I would give you a flying sofa
so you and Dad can ride anywhere.

I would give you a pile of leaves
so we can jump in together!"

Mum was so happy when she heard Piglet's
poem, she had to blow her nose.

"It's a thank you surprise because you helped
paint my bedroom, even when I was grumpy," said Piglet.

"Well, thank YOU," said Mum. "I love you.
And I love the poems you think up with your amazing imagination.
They say big things in little ways."

Then Dad got home and Piglet told him,
"You have to see how my bedroom is!"

So they all went upstairs.

And if footsteps could be happy, theirs were.

AN I-WOULD-GIVE-YOU POEM

Piglet's 'thank you surprise' for his mum was an I-WOULD-GIVE-YOU poem. It's a lovely kind of poem to write.

If you want to write one, the first thing you need to do is think of a person to give your poem to.

Perhaps there's someone you would like to say *thank you* to. Perhaps you'd like to write an I-WOULD-GIVE-YOU poem for someone's birthday, or Mother's Day or Father's Day, or another day when you might give someone a present.

One way or another, you'll write the best kind of I-WOULD-GIVE-YOU poem if you're writing it for a person you love, or who is special to you.

When you have chosen your person, you can write a poem like Piglet did.

Start each line with the words I WOULD GIVE YOU. And it's up to you how many lines long you make your poem.

Think about things your person would like, and choose one for each line. For example, Piglet starts his poem saying,

> I would give you a cup of tea with ginger biscuits.

A cup of tea and ginger biscuits are real things. You could actually give them to someone. But, like Piglet, you might also make your poem surprising. In that case, don't just pick real things to give. Do some extra thinking and imagine things you'd like to give which are not real.

Piglet says,

> I would give you a flying sofa so you and Dad can ride anywhere.

That's not real. But it's a special, and surprising, present.

In a poem you can invent any sort of fantastical gift if you want.

And remember, the more carefully you think about what your person would like, the more wonderful your imagined gifts will be. And the more magic there will be in your poem.

WRITING SECRETS

Two really good lines will make a better poem than twenty-two lines that have been written in a hurry and without putting special thinking into your words.

Piglet imagines his I-WOULD-GIVE-YOU poem 'word by word'. That's a good way to write. Don't worry about the whole thing. Work it out word by word, one line at a time, and slowly it will get written.

There aren't many things that you can give to somebody and keep at the same time. But a poem is one of them!

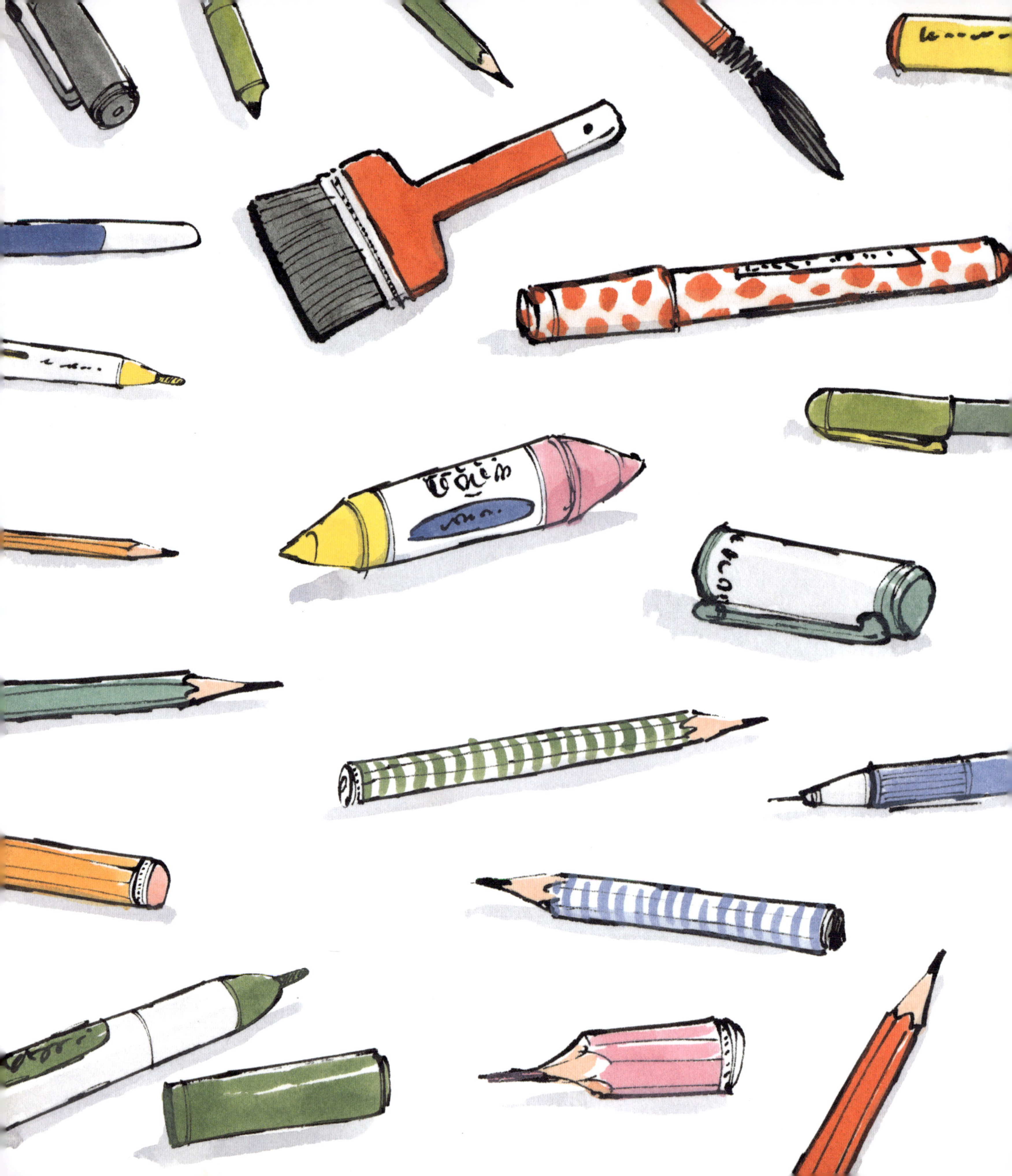

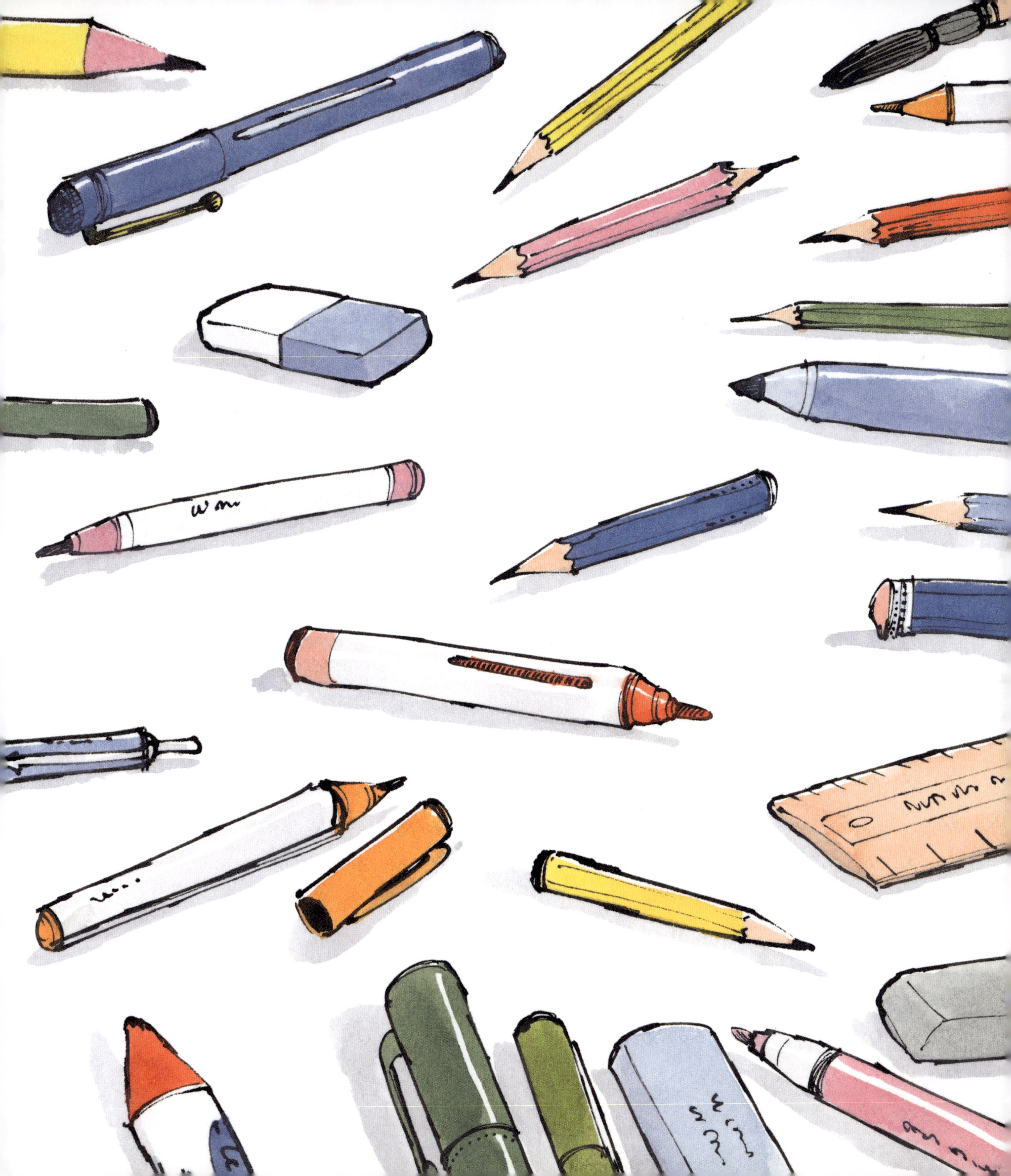

Write one word.

Then write another.

Write to remember.

And write to discover.